PEOPLE
on the Move

By Maddalen Esposito

CELEBRATION PRESS
Pearson Learning Group

Contents

Many people moved to live in the United States at the beginning of the twentieth century.

People Here, There, and Everywhere

There are very few places on this planet where people don't live. People have settled almost everywhere. Many of these people left their homes for another place or country. Why did they move?

People moved for different reasons. Many people moved to find better land, a better life, or more freedom. Some looked for wealth and some wanted adventure. Others were forced to move from their homelands. The following histories show that every time a group of people moved to a new place they changed the world.

This family left their homeland in 1968 to begin a new life in a new place.

The Travels of the Vikings

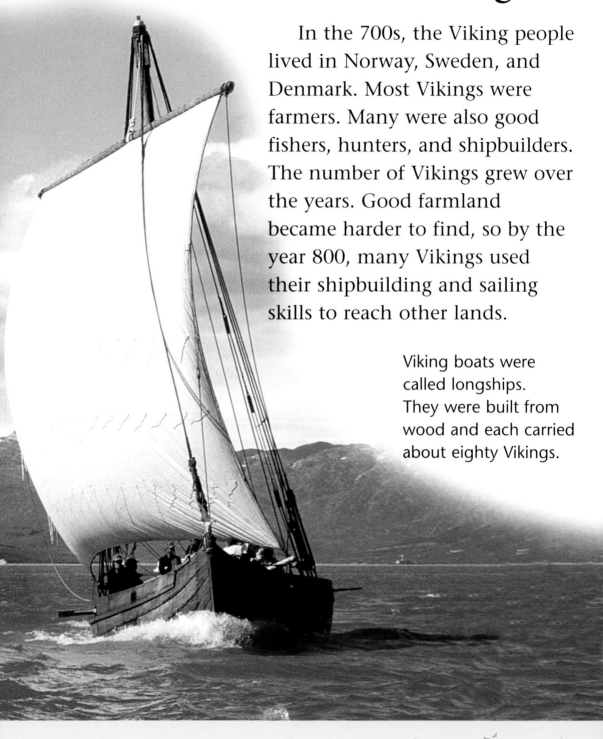

In the 700s, the Viking people lived in Norway, Sweden, and Denmark. Most Vikings were farmers. Many were also good fishers, hunters, and shipbuilders. The number of Vikings grew over the years. Good farmland became harder to find, so by the year 800, many Vikings used their shipbuilding and sailing skills to reach other lands.

Viking boats were called longships. They were built from wood and each carried about eighty Vikings.

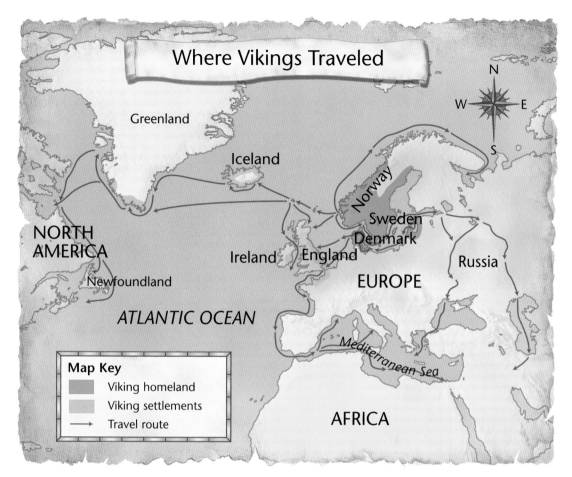

Where Vikings Traveled

Greenland

Iceland

Norway

Sweden

Denmark

NORTH AMERICA

Ireland England

Russia

Newfoundland

EUROPE

ATLANTIC OCEAN

Mediterranean Sea

Map Key
- Viking homeland
- Viking settlements
- → Travel route

AFRICA

Vikings covered long distances in their travels from 800 to 1100. Some of their journeys took many months.

Many Vikings made a living as traders in the new lands. They traded furs, timber, cloth, and gold with people in such places as England, Ireland, Russia, and the Middle East. Some became pirates. They were fierce fighters who raided cities, churches, and farms. Vikings had faster ships and better weapons than the people they attacked.

Vikings were skilled at using wood to build houses and boats.

Many Vikings settled in these faraway lands. Some did not return to their home because they found good farmland and more trading opportunities in the new lands. Other Vikings stayed because they wanted their own kingdom to rule. Sometimes they would remain in one place for so long that it became their new home.

When people move, they take their ideas and way of life with them. This is true of the Vikings. Many towns where Viking traders settled became trading centers and Viking shipbuilding skills spread around the world.

Viking trader

The Canadian Fur Trade

A fashion craze helped bring settlers to Canada. In the 1600s, people in Europe wanted fur for their clothes. Fur was used to make coats, hats, and decorative trim. There was a large beaver population in Canada, so the Europeans could buy their fur cheaply. The Native Americans hunted the beavers and traded the fur for blankets, cloth, guns, and fishing gear.

This woman wore a beaver-felt hat with ostrich feathers.

Large European companies sent traders to North America to try to control the fur trade.

A Native American hunter displays furs at a Canadian trading post.

European traders set up trading posts where hunters could exchange their goods. The traders told people back home about Canada. It had plenty of animals, fish, and lumber. It also had rich land for farming.

Soon settlements grew up around the trading posts. Many Native Americans lost their land to the Europeans who came to live there. Some of these settlements grew into the cities now known as Quebec, Montreal, and Winnipeg.

The North American Beaver
The beaver has had more influence on Canada than most animals. Today, the beaver is Canada's national animal. Laws in North America protect it from being overtrapped.

A Harsh Life in Australia

Sometimes people are forced to move to a new land. Many people who traveled to Australia in the 1700s had no choice. They were convicts, or people serving a prison sentence.

There was a large amount of crime in Great Britain's cities, so strict laws were put into place by the government. People could be sent to prison for owing money or stealing food. The prisons were already crowded, and there was little room for more prisoners. Many prisoners were kept on prison ships.

Prison ships like these on the Thames River in Great Britain were filled with prisoners.

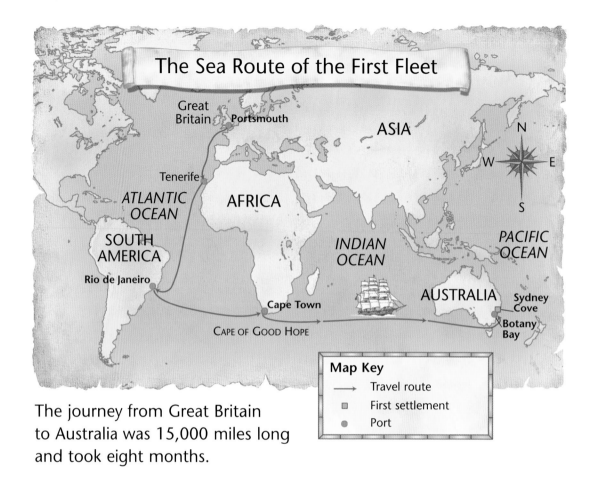

The Sea Route of the First Fleet

Great Britain · Portsmouth

ASIA

Tenerife

ATLANTIC OCEAN

AFRICA

SOUTH AMERICA

INDIAN OCEAN

PACIFIC OCEAN

Rio de Janeiro

Cape Town

AUSTRALIA · Sydney Cove

CAPE OF GOOD HOPE

Botany Bay

N W E S

Map Key
→ Travel route
▫ First settlement
● Port

The journey from Great Britain to Australia was 15,000 miles long and took eight months.

The British government decided to send convicts to Australia. On May 13, 1787, eight ships left Portsmouth, Great Britain, for Botany Bay, Australia. These ships were called the First Fleet. When the fleet arrived in Botany Bay, they discovered it had no fresh water. Fresh water was needed to establish a settlement, so the ships sailed on to Sydney Cove.

Life for the convicts was harsh. They had to build shelter and grow food in a strange land. Many crops failed, and many of the prisoners and soldiers starved.

Soldiers guarded the convict camps.

Eventually, a great number of people left Great Britain for Australia, including more than 100,000 convicts. Some convicts were freed and given land of their own. Many of the newcomers were free settlers. They traveled to Australia to start a new life. Together, these people helped settle Australia's largest city, Sydney, and Hobart, in the island state of Tasmania. Australia's Aboriginal people lost much of their land to the newcomers.

Sydney Harbour
Beautiful Sydney Harbour is Australia's main port. Captain Arthur Phillip named Sydney Cove after Viscount Sydney. He was the British Secretary of State when Captain James Cook claimed Australia for Great Britain in 1770.

The California Gold Rush

Would you be willing to move if it could make you rich? That's what happened in the United States in 1849. That year, news spread that gold was easy to find in California. People dropped everything to rush there. They left their homes and families behind. People traveled to California from all over the United States. They also sailed from faraway places such as China, Peru, Sweden, France, and Australia.

Forty-Niners
Men who went to California in 1849 to mine for gold were known as Forty-Niners. They came from farms, small villages, and cities. They crossed mountains, deserts, and oceans to try to strike it rich.

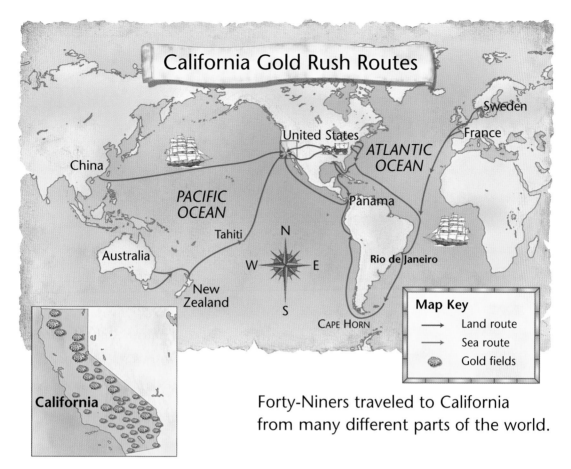

California Gold Rush Routes

China
United States
ATLANTIC OCEAN
Sweden
France
PACIFIC OCEAN
Panama
Tahiti
Australia
New Zealand
Rio de Janeiro
CAPE HORN

California

Map Key
→ Land route
→ Sea route
⬤ Gold fields

Forty-Niners traveled to California
from many different parts of the world.

    The journey to California was difficult. Railroads from the east of the United States ran only about halfway across the country. After traveling by train, people walked beside their wagons for the rest of the way. This part of the journey was more than 2,000 miles.

    Other people from the east of the United States and Europe sailed on ships around Cape Horn at the southern tip of South America. The journey was dangerous and it often took six months to get to California. Still, more than 80,000 people arrived in California in just one year.

Americans and Chinese worked side by side in the gold fields.

Goldminers washed earth or gravel in a pan searching for gold. This was called panning.

gold nuggets

Very few people became rich. The Gold Rush, however, changed California forever. The rush to find riches helped open up the American West to more settlers. As a result, many Native Americans lost their land. California grew quickly and became a state in 1850. Most miners expected to return home with gold, but many decided to stay in California. The state became home to people of every color and many backgrounds.

We're Still on the Move

Today, people continue to settle in new places. Like the Vikings, they may be looking for new land or adventure. Like the fur traders and the Forty-Niners, they may be looking for new or better opportunities, or like the convicts, they may be forced to leave their homes. As long as people continue to move, the world will continue changing.

Index